The 12 Days Of Christmas Song

A Festive Coloring Book

This Book Belongs To:

_____

Copyright © 2022 Anna Nadler
All rights reserved
Published by Anna Nadler Art
No part of this publication may be
reproduced, stored in a retrieval system or
transmitted in any form or by any means,
electronic, mechanical, photocopying, recording
or otherwise, without prior written permission
from the author/publisher.
www.annanadlerart.com

ISBN: 9781958428207

On the first day
Of Christmas
My true love
Sent to me:
A Partridge
In a Pear Tree

On the second
Day of Christmas
My true love
Sent to me:
2 Turtle Doves
And a Partridge
In a Pear Tree

On the third day
Of Christmas
My true love
Sent to me:
3 French Hens
2 Turtle Doves
And a Partridge
In a Pear Tree

On the fifth
Day of Christmas
My true love
Sent to me:
5 Golden Rings
4 Calling Birds
3 French Hens
2 Turtle Doves
And a Partridge
In a Pear Tree

On the sixth
Day of Christmas
My true love
Sent to me:
6 Geese a Laying
5 Golden Rings
4 Calling Birds
3 French Hens
2 Turtle Doves
And a Partridge
In a Pear Tree

On the seventh
Day of Christmas
My true love
Sent to me:
7 Swans a Swimming
6 Geese a Laying
5 Golden Rings
4 Calling Birds
3 French Hens
2 Turtle Doves
And a Partridge
In a Pear Tree

On the ninth
Day of Christmas
My true love
Sent to me:
9 Ladies Dancing
8 Maids a Milking
7 Swans a Swimming
6 Geese a Laying
5 Golden Rings
4 Calling Birds
3 French Hens
2 Turtle Doves
And a Partridge
In a Pear Tree

On the tenth
Day of Christmas
My true love sent to me:
10 Lords a Leaping
9 Ladies Dancing
8 Maids a Milking
7 Swans a Swimming
6 Geese a Laying
5 Golden Rings
4 Calling Birds
3 French Hens
2 Turtle Doves
And a Partridge
In a Pear Tree

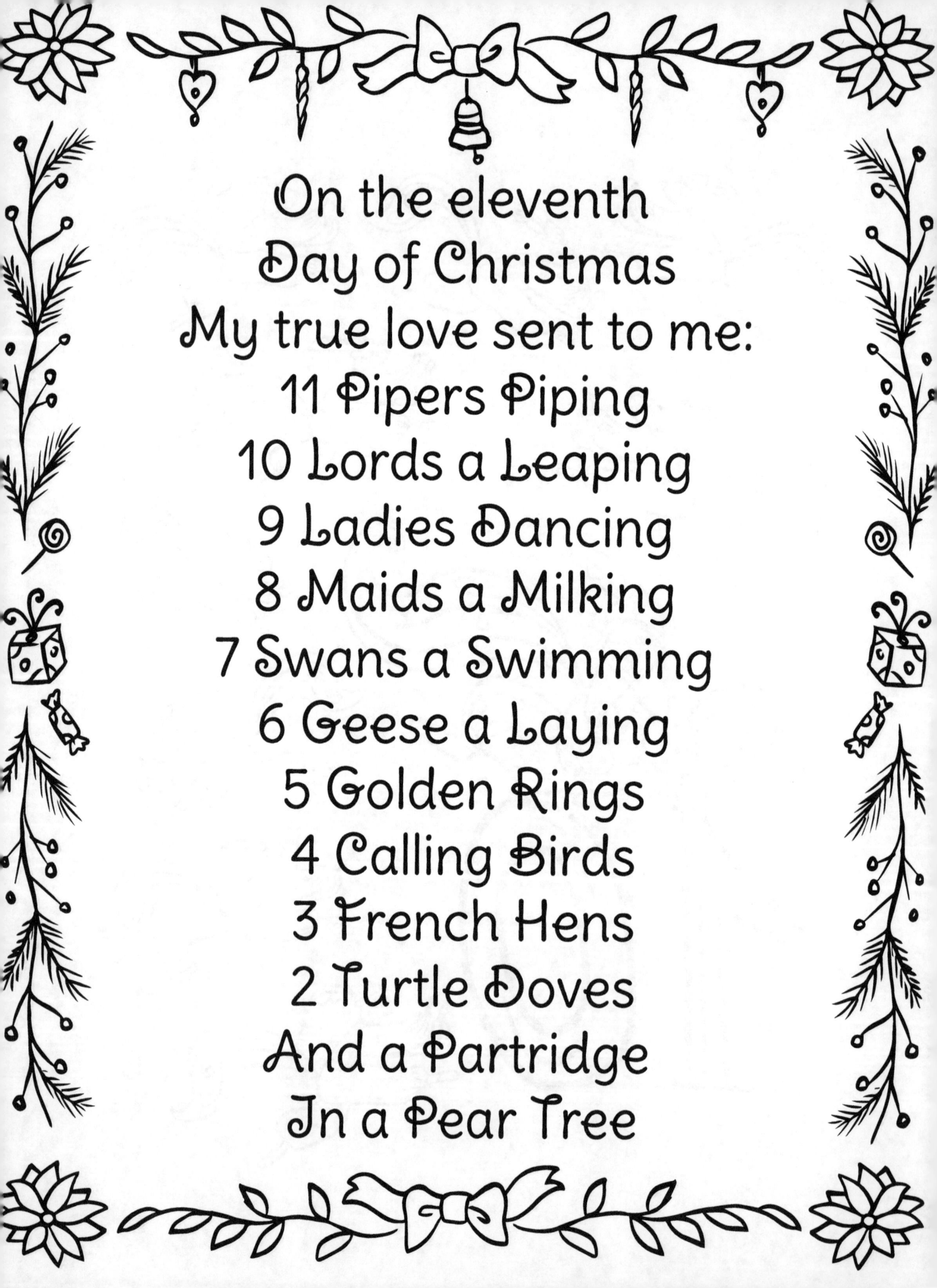

On the eleventh
Day of Christmas
My true love sent to me:
11 Pipers Piping
10 Lords a Leaping
9 Ladies Dancing
8 Maids a Milking
7 Swans a Swimming
6 Geese a Laying
5 Golden Rings
4 Calling Birds
3 French Hens
2 Turtle Doves
And a Partridge
In a Pear Tree

On the twelfth day of Christmas
My true love sent to me:
12 Drummers Drumming
11 Pipers Piping
10 Lords a Leaping
9 Ladies Dancing
8 Maids a Milking
7 Swans a Swimming
6 Geese a Laying
5 Golden Rings
4 Calling Birds
3 French Hens
2 Turtle Doves
And a Partridge
In a Pear Tree

On the first day
Of Christmas
My true love
Sent to me:
A Partridge
In a Pear Tree

On the second
Day of Christmas
My true love
Sent to me:
2 Turtle Doves
And a Partridge
In a Pear Tree

On the third day
Of Christmas
My true love
Sent to me:
3 French Hens
2 Turtle Doves
And a Partridge
In a Pear Tree

On the fourth
Day of Christmas
My true love
Sent to me:
4 Calling Birds
3 French Hens
2 Turtle Doves
And a Partridge
In a Pear Tree

On the fifth
Day of Christmas
My true love
Sent to me:
5 Golden Rings
4 Calling Birds
3 French Hens
2 Turtle Doves
And a Partridge
In a Pear Tree

On the sixth
Day of Christmas
My true love
Sent to me:
6 Geese a Laying
5 Golden Rings
4 Calling Birds
3 French Hens
2 Turtle Doves
And a Partridge
In a Pear Tree

On the seventh
Day of Christmas
My true love
Sent to me:
7 Swans a Swimming
6 Geese a Laying
5 Golden Rings
4 Calling Birds
3 French Hens
2 Turtle Doves
And a Partridge
In a Pear Tree

On the eighth
Day of Christmas
My true love
Sent to me:
8 Maids a Milking
7 Swans a Swimming
6 Geese a Laying
5 Golden Rings
4 Calling Birds
3 French Hens
2 Turtle Doves
And a Partridge
In a Pear Tree

On the ninth
Day of Christmas
My true love
Sent to me:
9 Ladies Dancing
8 Maids a Milking
7 Swans a Swimming
6 Geese a Laying
5 Golden Rings
4 Calling Birds
3 French Hens
2 Turtle Doves
And a Partridge
In a Pear Tree

On the tenth
Day of Christmas
My true love sent to me:
10 Lords a Leaping
9 Ladies Dancing
8 Maids a Milking
7 Swans a Swimming
6 Geese a Laying
5 Golden Rings
4 Calling Birds
3 French Hens
2 Turtle Doves
And a Partridge
In a Pear Tree

On the eleventh
Day of Christmas
My true love sent to me:
11 Pipers Piping
10 Lords a Leaping
9 Ladies Dancing
8 Maids a Milking
7 Swans a Swimming
6 Geese a Laying
5 Golden Rings
4 Calling Birds
3 French Hens
2 Turtle Doves
And a Partridge
In a Pear Tree

On the twelfth day of Christmas
My true love sent to me:
12 Drummers Drumming
11 Pipers Piping
10 Lords a Leaping
9 Ladies Dancing
8 Maids a Milking
7 Swans a Swimming
6 Geese a Laying
5 Golden Rings
4 Calling Birds
3 French Hens
2 Turtle Doves
And a Partridge
In a Pear Tree

We hope you loved this festive coloring book!
It is an illustrated rendition of the classic song - "The 12 Days of Christmas."
It has cute characters who are fun, whimsical, funny, joyful and playful.
You will see squirrels, mice, a cow, dogs, cats, rabbits, different birds and more, dressed up in holiday outfits!
The lyrics to the song are included on each opposite page, next to the drawings.
Sing along as you color this wonderful book!
We have included 2 sets of these pictures, so you can color and sing twice!

Thank you for coloring this book and singing along!

If you enjoyed it, feel free to leave a review!